PLANETS

VENUS

Alexis Roumanis

LET'S READ
AV2 BY WEIGL™
ADDED VALUE • AUDIO VISUAL

www.av2books.com

LET'S READ

AV²
BY WEIGL™

ADDED VALUE • AUDIO VISUAL

Go to **www.av2books.com**, and enter this book's unique code.

BOOK CODE

T249489

AV² by Weigl brings you media enhanced books that support active learning.

AV² provides enriched content that supplements and complements this book. Weigl's AV² books strive to create inspired learning and engage young minds in a total learning experience.

Your AV² Media Enhanced books come alive with...

Audio
Listen to sections of the book read aloud.

Video
Watch informative video clips.

Embedded Weblinks
Gain additional information for research.

Try This!
Complete activities and hands-on experiments.

Key Words
Study vocabulary, and complete a matching word activity.

Quizzes
Test your knowledge.

Slide Show
View images and captions, and prepare a presentation.

... and much, much more!

Published by AV² by Weigl
350 5ᵗʰ Avenue, 59ᵗʰ Floor New York, NY 10118
Websites: www.av2books.com   www.weigl.com

Library of Congress Cataloging-in-Publication Data

Roumanis, Alexis, author.
Venus / Alexis Roumanis.
     pages cm. -- (Planets)
Includes index.
ISBN 978-1-4896-3308-8 (hard cover : alk. paper) -- ISBN 978-1-4896-3309-5 (soft cover : alk. paper) -- ISBN 978-1-4896-3310-1 (single user ebook) -- ISBN 978-1-4896-3311-8 (multi-user ebook)
1. Venus (Planet)--Juvenile literature. I. Title.
QB621.R68 2016
523.42--dc23
                    2014041610

Printed in the United States of America in Brainerd, Minnesota
1 2 3 4 5 6 7 8 9 0 19 18 17 16 15

022015
WEP081214

Project Coordinator: Katie Gillespie Art Director: Terry Paulhus

Weigl acknowledges Getty Images and iStock as the primary image suppliers for this title.

VENUS

CONTENTS

What Is Venus?

Venus is a planet. It moves in a path around the Sun. Venus is the second planet from the Sun.

Sun

Mercury

Venus

Earth

Mars

Ceres

Jupiter

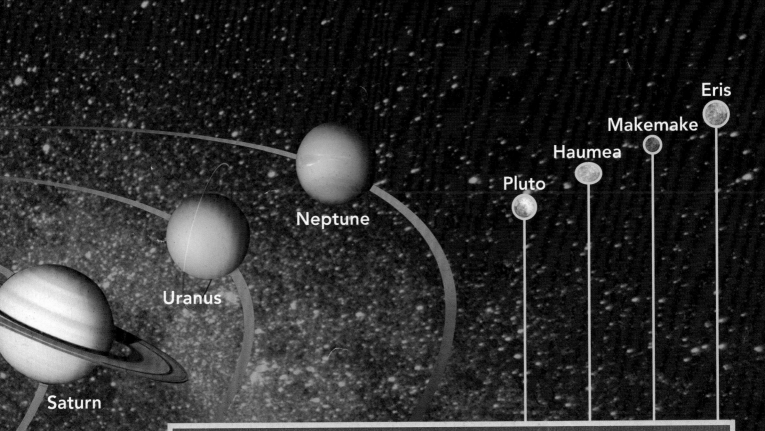

Eris

Makemake

Haumea

Pluto

Neptune

Uranus

Saturn

Dwarf Planets

Dwarf planets are round objects that move around the Sun. Unlike planets, they share their part of space with other objects.

How Big Is Venus?

Venus is the third smallest planet in the solar system. It is almost as big as Earth.

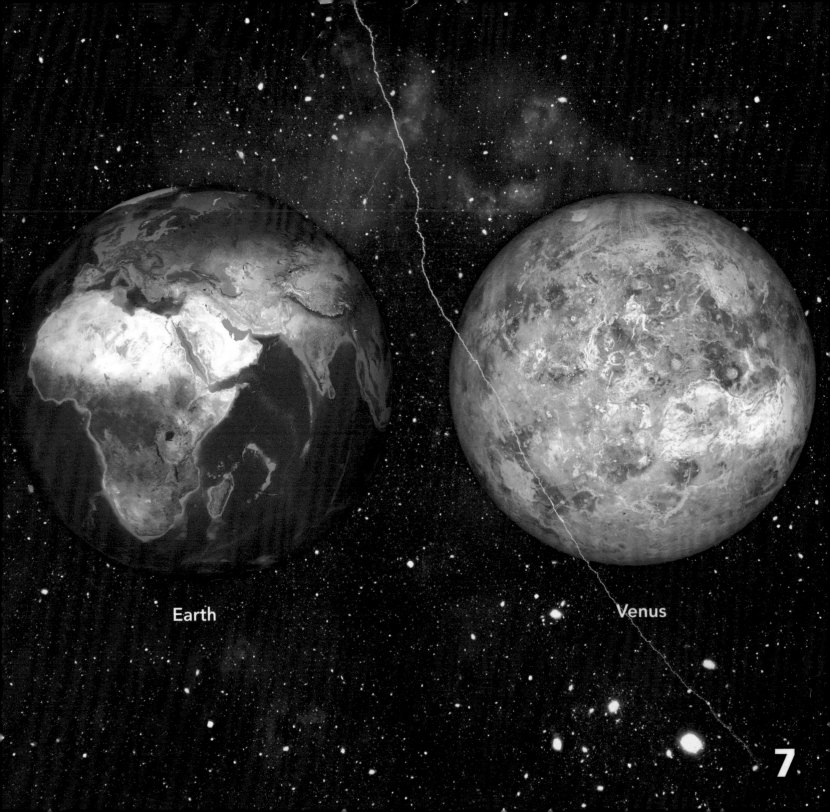

Earth

Venus

7

What Is Venus Made Of?

Venus is a rocky planet.
It has many large volcanoes.
Venus is covered in rocks
from these volcanoes.

9

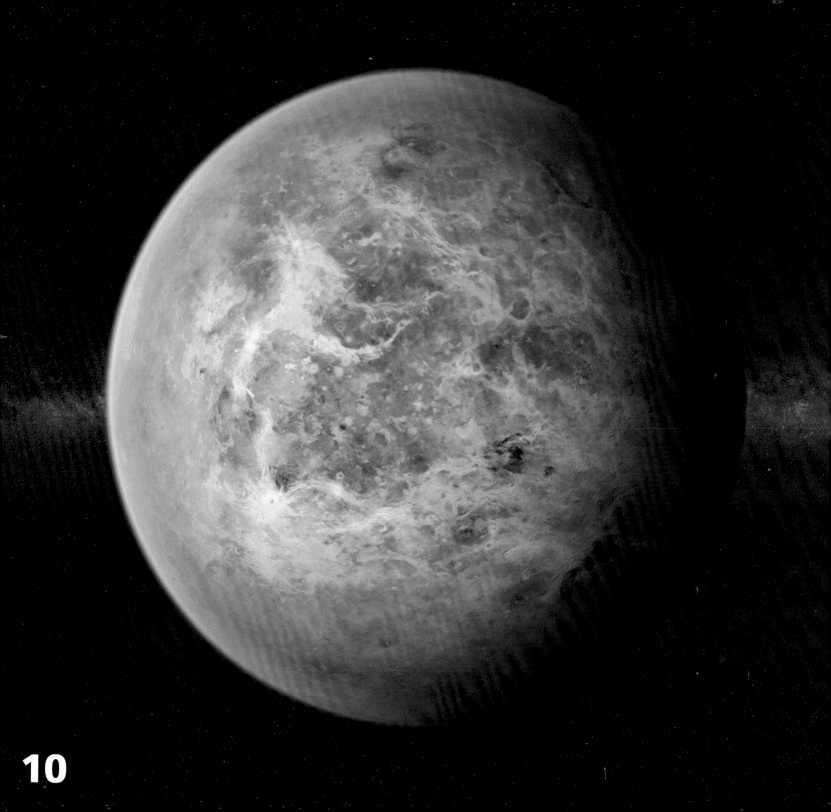

What Does Venus Look Like?

Thick clouds cover the whole planet. These clouds make Venus look yellow.

What Is Maat Mons?

Maat Mons is a volcano on Venus. It is the highest volcano on the planet. Maat Mons is about the same size as the island of Hawai'i.

13

Venus

Mercury

Who First Studied Venus?

The Maya first studied Venus
thousands of years ago.
They built a calendar based
on how Venus moved.

Venus's Missing Moon

Venus has no moon. Mercury is the only other planet without a moon. Mercury may once have been Venus's moon.

18

How Is Venus Different from Earth?

All planets spin. Venus spins much more slowly than Earth. Venus and Earth also spin in different directions.

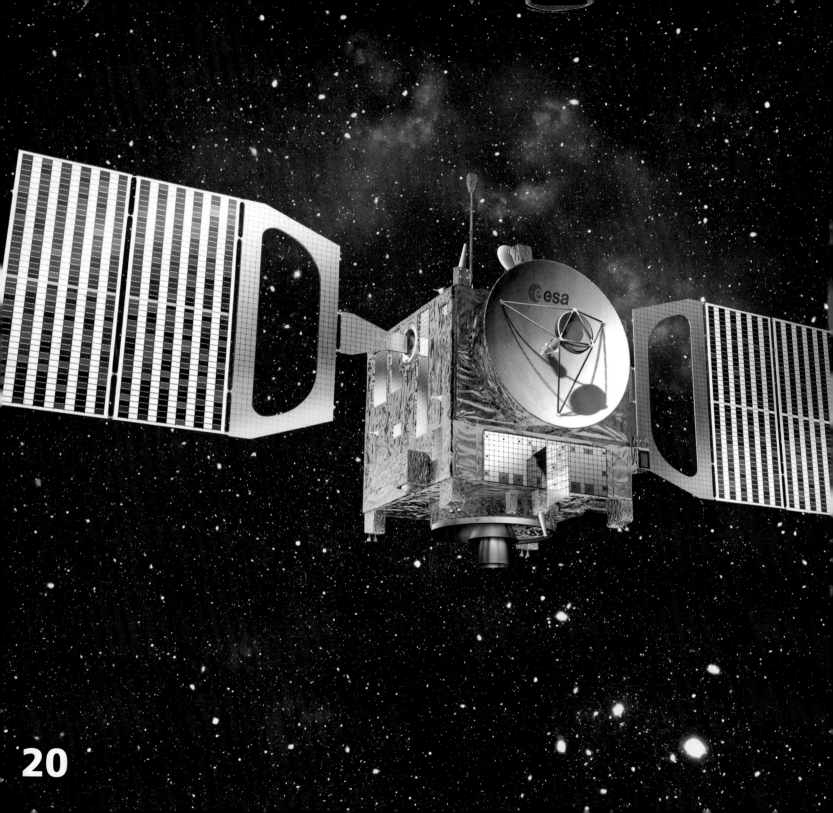

How Do We Learn about Venus Today?

Scientists send vehicles called probes into space to study the solar system. A space probe called *Venus Express* went to Venus in 2005. It arrived in 2006 and is still used to study the planet today.

VENUS FACTS

This page provides more detail about the interesting facts found in the book. They are intended to be used by adults as a learning support to help young readers round out their knowledge of each planet featured in the *Planets* series.

Pages 4–5

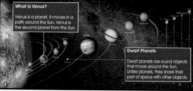

Venus is a planet. Planets are round objects that move around, or orbit, a star, with enough mass to clear smaller objects from their orbit. Earth's solar system has eight planets, five known dwarf planets, and many other space objects that all orbit the Sun. Venus is 67 million miles (108 million kilometers) from the Sun. It takes 225 Earth days for Venus to make one orbit around the Sun.

Pages 6–7

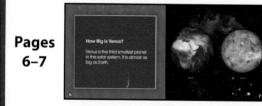

Venus is the third smallest planet in the solar system. Gravity is a force that pulls objects toward a planet's center. The force of gravity is almost the same on Venus as it is on Earth. A 100-pound (45-kilogram) object on Earth would weigh 91 pounds (41 kg) on Venus.

Pages 8–9

Venus is a rocky planet. Thousands of volcanoes can be found on the surface of Venus. Lava flows have created channels that spread out like rivers. The planet's surface is also covered in volcanic rock. An atmosphere is made up of gases that surround a planet. Volcanic activity over thousands of years has created a thick atmosphere around Venus.

Pages 10–11

Thick clouds cover the whole planet. Venus has a cloud layer that is about 12.4 miles (20 km) thick. The cloud layer is mostly made up of sulfuric acid. This makes the planet look yellow. Acid rain falls from the clouds, but does not reach the ground. High temperatures evaporate the rain before it can hit the ground. Moving clouds help to shape the planet's surface.

Pages 12–13

Maat Mons is a volcano on Venus. It is a shield volcano. Shield volcanoes are formed by lava flowing out of the volcano in all directions. Lava usually flows quickly out of shield volcanoes. Maat Mons is about 5 miles (8 km) high. The largest shield volcano on Earth is called Mauna Loa. It is only 2.5 miles (4 km) above sea level.

Pages 14–15

Venus has no moon. Some scientists believe that Mercury was once Venus's moon, but it broke away from Venus's orbit. This may explain why neither planet has a moon. Venus was also once thought to have a different moon, named Neith. Many astronomers thought that they saw Neith. Today, it is believed that what they actually saw was a star.

Pages 16–17

The Maya first studied Venus thousands of years ago. They believed that Venus and the Sun were brothers because they both rise and set around the same time. Mayan astronomers observed Venus for several years before creating their calendar. It had a year of 365 days, as calendars do today.

Pages 18–19

All planets spin. This is called rotation. The time it takes for a planet to complete one rotation on its axis is the length of a day. On Earth, this takes 24 hours. One day on Venus is 5,832 hours. Some scientists think that Venus used to spin in the same direction as Earth. Many years ago, Venus's axis may have flipped 180 degrees. This would mean that Venus spins the same way it always did, just upside down.

Pages 20–21

Scientists send vehicles called probes into space to study the solar system. *Venus Express* was built by the European Space Agency. It arrived in orbit around Venus in April 2006. Since then, it has helped discover that Venus is likely still geologically active. This means that the surface of the planet is still changing, due to the weather, climate, quakes, and volcanoes.

KEY WORDS

Research has shown that as much as 65 percent of all written material published in English is made up of 300 words. These 300 words cannot be taught using pictures or learned by sounding them out. They must be recognized by sight. This book contains 60 common sight words to help young readers improve their reading fluency and comprehension. This book also teaches young readers several important content words. These words are paired with pictures to aid in learning and improve understanding.

Page	Sight Words First Appearance
4	a, around, from, in, is, it, moves, second, the, what
5	are, of, other, part, that, their, they, with
6	almost, as, big, Earth, how
8	has, large, made, many, these
11	does, like, look, make
12	about, on, same
15	been, have, may, once, only, without
16	first, who, years
19	all, also, and, different, more, much, than
21	do, into, learn, still, study, to, used, we, went

Page	Content Words First Appearance
4	path, planet, Sun, Venus
5	dwarf planets, objects, space
6	solar system
8	rocks, volcanoes
11	clouds, yellow
12	Hawai'i, island, Maat Mons, size
15	Mercury, moon
16	calendar, Maya
21	probes, scientists, vehicles, *Venus Express*